Cure Depression Without Drugs For Good

AJ Barrington

Over the past year or so I have tried to research a gentleman by the name of Henry James Rivers, who, more than 50 years ago wrote a book entitled "The Rivers Course of Nerve Treatment".

I purchased a Copy of this course in 1964 in desperation to find a cure for my severe depression and self-harming tendencies.

I still have the course today as they were priceless to me all those years ago.

I know there are many men and women at the present time suffering from nervous disorders that could benefit from Mr. Rivers course of treatment.

Mr Rivers worked in Huntingdon (Cambs) in the 60's and if any family member or business partner wishes to contact me to discuss any issues regarding the publication of this course, would they kindly contact me through the publishers.

Thank You.

When Dad told my Brother and I that he wanted to publish a book it wasn't a surprise.

He always had lots of dreams and ambitions and this was just another one on his list.

No, the surprise was the subject of the book. During our early years there was never a hint of the difficulties he went through all those years ago. Never any self pity or bitterness just a loving and happy family.

Hopefully this book will not only allow you to firstly cure yourself, but help you to go on and achieve YOUR dreams, whatever they may be.

Trevor

When I was in my 20's I had a major intestinal operation which left me with severe depression and suicidal tendencies which seemed to get worse by each day.

I struggled through the days trying to carry out my work, and not wanting to worry my Parents, I kept all my thoughts to myself which made my situation even worse.

I visited my Doctor on many occasions who readily prescribed anti-depressant tablets which I was pleased to take 3 or 4 times a day as they seem to relieve my depression for a short while. As my condition did not seem to improve my Doctor then suggested he made an appointment for me to see a psychiatrist which I promptly declined, and left his surgery feeling even worse than before. In my heart I knew taking anti-depressant tablets would not cure me, but had no choice but to keep on swallowing them.

Shortly after this I noticed an advertisement in a magazine I had bought which would completely change my life and how I thought.

A gentleman by the name of Henry James Rivers was advertising his booklets on how to cure Depression & other related illnesses entitled "The Rivers Course of Nerve Treatment", which suggested I could cure my problem using his simple method.

In desperation I sent off for the course thinking it would be a complete waste of money.

When the booklets arrived I started reading them right away and after a while I remember thinking it all seems too simple to cure my many problems and feelings.

How wrong I was.

As I read on, it began to dawn on me that Mr Rivers method wasn't so silly as I had first thought, and it gradually became compelling reading, and that many illnesses could be cured by AUTO-SUGGESTION.

In simple terms instead of telling yourself all day how "terrible you feel" and I shall "never get better" as I did, through simple exercises that you read to yourself for just a few minutes twice a day you can gradually change negative thoughts, usually over a period of just a few weeks, to positive thoughts as your brain gradually excepts the new suggestions until you are fully cured, and your will power is restored to its former level before you became depressed. That, in simple terms, is what Auto-Suggestion is.

If your problem is depression for instance I would imagine you are taking anti-depressant tablets, your friends telling you to "pull yourself together", telling yourself continually "how terrible you feel", and your friends "don't understand" all help to "run down" your WILL POWER with your brain powerless not to accept these negative thoughts.

This simple treatment would follow a similar course if you were suffering from Anxiety, Worry, Fear of becoming insane, Insomnia, Imaginary fears or if you wanted to stop smoking etc.

Just refer to Mr Rivers suggestion table at the rear of this book to suit your particular problem.

(You could even make up your own suggestion table for your particular need)

Please let me make it quite clear I do not profess to know in scientific terms how Auto-Suggestion works, neither do you have to.

YOU SIMPLY HAVE TO BELIEVE IT.

Before I pass you over to the expert to explain in simple terms more about how Auto-Suggestion works, may I just say this.

If after a few days of carrying out the exercises, you do not seem to feel any better, please do not stop. Carry on with renewed energy and belief and your WILL

POWER will gradually get stronger and stronger, and your old negative thoughts that were so destructive will get weaker and weaker.

As far as I was concerned it seemed impossible when I was at my lowest point to think about fulfilling ambitions that I had as a boy, but after I was cured I had renewed will power, energy and determination that filled me with excitement. So much so in 1974 with 2 Sons age 6 and 3 and very little money I decided to start my own business.

As I never thought it could fail, and with my Wife's help, the business thrived until 2002 when I retired, at least from full-time work.

You may not want to do anything like I did. You may have always wanted to say, manufacture something you thought of some years ago but never thought it would be successful, or perhaps do something amazing for charity.

Feel the new blood course through your body giving you new energy, positive thoughts and exciting prospects for the future, your family, your whole life.

Mr Henry Rivers cured himself from his disorders and wrote these self-help booklets for others to benefit.

I sincerely hope they benefit <u>you</u> as much as they have me.

I would very much like you to keep in touch with me and any questions you may have. I will do my best to answer them, and remember: DON'T SAY YOU CAN'T , SAY YOU <u>CAN</u> AND YOU WILL

And

AS A MAN THINKETH SO SHALL HE BECOME (The same, of course, applies to women)

My Sincere Best Wishes to you
Alan Barrington
<u>ambarrington@yahoo.co.uk</u>

PART 1

THE CAUSE of NERVOUS DISORDERS

LESSON 1

The Object of this Course

In writing this course of mental education I make no claim to literary ability but I do profess to know something of the laws of nature, particularly those appertaining to the attainment and preservation of mental and physical health.

In the first place, I want you to understand that I am writing for the benefit of sufferers in all walks of life, and, in order that my teaching may be perfectly clear to everyone of my readers, it will be necessary for me to express myself in a rather more elementary manner that I should adopt if this Course was written for medical students only. For this reason I must request the indulgence of many of my readers and ask them to kindly forgive me if I take some pains to explain points which may be perfectly obvious to them but which are by no means as clear to my less enlightened readers. After all, you are seeking help, not entertainment, and you need real practical advice, not technical phraseology, so if I call a spade a "spade" and not "an agricultural implement" every reader will understand me and we shall get along much better.

Throughout the Course I shall write only in the simplest language avoiding all medical and scientific terms, just as though you and I were having a friendly chat together, and using such expressions as I should adopt if we were actually in personal conversation.

I want you to pay particular attention to all sentences printed in bold type, especially where special display has been given to them. Read each of these sentences over and over again – they contain a volume of practical information and advice in a few telling words. By the way, although I shall address myself throughout the Course to male readers, I need hardly say that my teaching applies to both sexes.

THE NECESSITY OF CLOSE ATTENTION. I want to ask you not to read any further unless you have time to give me your closest attention. This is not an ordinary book to be glanced through casually, but a course of treatment which should be read and studied earnestly and carefully so that you are able to thoroughly grasp all that I am going to teach you. It is not my intention to write an educational treatise, explaining only the nature and peculiarities of nervous disorders, but I am going to tell you how to cure your complaint as well as what it is ; I am going to make my Course instructive as well as interesting. You will therefore appreciate the necessity of giving your whole mind to the subject we are about to investigate and you cannot do so unless you have plenty of time to spare.

Presuming that you have an hour or two of leisure, I suggest that you retire to a private room, or somewhere where you are not likely to be disturbed, and then prepare to give me your very closest attention and I will teach you something that I earnestly hope will be the means of altering and improving the whole course of your life.

I advise you to first read the Course through, so that you can get a clear idea of its general character, and then return to the beginning and commence more earnest study, making sure that you thoroughly understand each lesson before going on to the next one. After this careful study, which is in itself very beneficial, you should also carry out the special treatment which will be described later on.

Having now made ourselves familiar with each

other, let us settle back comfortably in our chairs and get ahead.

THE TASK BEFORE US. Now, before we proceed any further, let us thoroughly understand each other and the task we are about to endeavour to accomplish. Remember, my friend, that I used to be just as nervous as you are now, and, having succeeded in curing myself, I am going to strive my utmost to show you how you may become cured also. I have the greatest confidence in the belief that you can cure yourself and I want you to believe this too. However impossible it may at present seem to you, I am absolutely certain that every sufferer from the nervous complaints herein described can positively cure himself (or herself) by following the methods laid down in this Course.

At present you are, presumably, a highly-strung, nervous and over-sensitive individual. To make our task a success you must be transformed into a person of a bright and cheerful disposition without the slightest trace of nervousness in your character. A sheer impossibility you may think at present, but I am going to prove the contrary. In this age of enlightenment we are beginning to realise that we are something more than mere columns of flesh and blood and to appreciate the tremendous power of the mind over the body.

We are apt to overlook the important fact that our lives are greatly influenced by our mental attitude and that we are creators of our own personalities. As a man thinks, so shall he become. We are born into the world with certain gifts and faculties and whether we take full advantage of these God-given talents and develop them to their fullest extent, or allow them to remain dormant and unproductive all our lives, is dependant entirely upon ourselves. Success or failure, happiness or misery, health or illness are not necessarily qualities that are born within us ; they are all capable of being cultivated and developed by everyone. You are not nervous because the ability to be bold and fearless is missing from your personality – the quality of courage is within you alright, but you have allowed your self-created fears to gain such a firm hold upon you that the opposite qualities have become suppressed. It is only necessary to reverse your mental outlook and to realise that the qualities you desire are just as capable of development as the qualities you do not desire, to be able to bring the desire qualities uppermost in your personality.

"KNOWLEDGE IS POWER". The principal reason why we suffer illness is because we do not understand the nature of our complaints and we are therefore unqualified to cure them. I firmly believe in the maxim, "Knowledge is power," for had I not found out exactly what caused my nervous disposition and how to cure it I doubt if I should ever have become cured. A man cannot make a dynamo if he does not know what a dynamo is; neither can you cure your nervousness if you do not know what nervousness is. I am going to tell you in a few minutes valuable knowledge that it has taken me many years to learn, and I firmly believe that when once you understand what nervousness really is and why you are nervous you will be more than half cured!

The object of this Course is to give you the knowledge that is normally possessed only by doctors and to make you sufficiently competent to treat yourself as successfully as though you were in the hand of a skilled nerve-specialist. Until you know what is wrong with you, you cannot expect to become cured, but when I have explained everything to you, you will be delighted to find how easy it is to cure yourself and how great is the power of knowledge.

THE FUTILITY OF MEDICINE. I want to impress upon you the utter futility (and stupidity) of wasting money on advertised so-called "nerve-tonics" and other patent medicines in the attempt to cure nervous disorders. The market to-day is absolutely flooded with all kinds of these proprietary medicines, but instead of relieving the suffering of mankind their only achievement has been to turn us into a nation of pill-swallowing mollycoddles. It would be well for sufferers to realise that these patent medicines are manufactured on an enormous scale by big manufacturing chemists whose main object is to make money and not to cure illness. If the curative value of these remedies was as high as their proprietors assert, their effect would be to raise the standard of health to such a high level that there would eventually be practically no demand for patent medicines and the manufacturers would thus bring about their own ruin!

It must be remembered that the financial success of a patent medicine retailed at a small price depends entirely upon the customer purchasing a considerable quantity of the remedy, and the aim of the pill-merchant is not to effect rapid cure for a small outlay but to encourage the customer to continue taking the stuff as long as he is foolish enough to do so.

The huge and expensive advertising schemes organised by patent medicine manufacturers and the flattering so-called "testimonials" they publish (many being written by celebrities in all walks of life who are, of course, handsomely paid for writing them) induces the poor misguided sufferer to believe that there really must be some curative value in them, but I can honestly assure my readers that there is not a single patent medicine on the market that is capable of curing any form of nervous disorder without the aid of any other curative measures. The medicine that can cure a disordered mind does not exist – and never will!

MEDICINE CANNOT PERFORM MIRACLES. Those of my readers who have already wasted money on advertised medicines will need little convincing that such an experiment is usually fraught with disappointment and failure and that medicine alone cannot cure nervous disorders, but for the benefit of others who may not be quite convinced on this point I should like to explain in a few words just why drugs cannot cure you.

It is a difficult matter to convince nervous people that they are not physically ill and they do not require medicine at all. The fact that these nervous fears and forebodings have no physical basis and should not be treated as diseases is usually entirely overlooked by sufferers. In proving once and for all the sheer inadequacy of medicine to cure these nervous weaknesses, I wish to impress upon my reader the fact that their complaints are purely mental in origin and the administration of drugs in any shape or form cannot possibly reach the seat of the trouble, which is in the sufferer's mind. It is in the brain and nervous system that the fault lies and only by removing the cause from the mind can we succeed in curing these obstinate disorders.

The particular form of nervous disorders with which we are concerned are really a part of one's character – a weakness of character – rather than actual diseases, and they are just as much a phase of mental and nervous inefficiency as is a bad habit or a poor memory. To take medicine in an effort to cure these nerve troubles is as hopelessly inadequate as to try to eradicate by the same means a weak memory or a bad habit.

As the late Dr Andrew Wilson, in one of his works on the nervous system, truly said, "To attempt to cure nervousness by means of medicine would be as irrational a proceeding as to attempt to cure reflex crying in an infant, or to check the natural action of the skin. All these are physiological actions characteristic of health, or are, at least, associated with the healthy state, and therefore lie beyond the province of medicine altogether."

If you are at present taking any form of medicine for your complaint I should like you to give it up whilst undergoing my system of treatment – you will not require it afterwards!

WHY DOCTORS FAIL TO CURE. I do not wish you to presume from the foregoing remarks that I am opposed to the medical profession or that I wish to imply that we can do without doctors. I have the deepest respect for medical men and I fully realise that the great progress made in medical science is an immense boon to suffering humanity and deserving of the highest praise and gratitude. I do, however, believe that most of the patients who fill the consulting rooms of the ordinary family doctors day after day do not need medical attention at all and would get better much quicker – and cheaper – if they used their own brains a little more instead of relying so much on the "mollycoddling" treatment of their doctors.

After all, doctors are only human and they have to make a living, so we cannot blame them if they take your money and give you "treatment" when they know that there is really nothing organically wrong with you and that their medicine cannot do you much good. It is really so much easier for your doctor to give you a bottle of mysterious medicine and to bundle you out of his consulting room, than to spend an hour or so in giving you a candid lecture that would convince you that your trouble is of your own creation and that you could do yourself far more good than he could – especially when his waiting room is full of other "dying ducks" waiting to give him money for nothing!

The overworked family doctor has neither the time nor the inclination (nor, in many cases, the ability) to give each patient the individual care and attention that is really essential to effect a satisfactory cure where intricate nervous disorders are concerned. It is in this respect that a course of treatment such as this succeeds where doctors fail, for, instead of giving you a box of pills or a bottle of medicine and saying, "This will soon put you right," and then hoping for the best, I actually tell you what is wrong with you (which a doctor seldom does) and explain exactly what you must do to get well.

Most of the medicine made up by private doctors and distributed wholesale amongst their patients, no matter from what they may suffer, consists for the most part merely of coloured water. The patient deludes himself with the belief that the wonderful medicine will cure him and it sometimes does, but he does not realise that only his own faith and not the medicine has cured him. (This faith in the curative value of useless medicine is really Auto-Suggestion, about which you will learn more presently).

LESSON II

The Analysis of Nervous Disorders

The rush and excitement of modern life, with its resultant strain on the nervous system of the individual, has rewarded us with numerous disorders of a kind which were almost unknown a few generations ago. Most of these mental and nervous disorders may be grouped under the general heading of what we term Neurasthenia. Neurasthenia ailments almost invariably have the same characteristics in that they arise from the imagination of the sufferer and have little or no physical basis.

The sufferer from Neurasthenia is not necessarily a physical weakling, but the over-excited and super-sensitive condition of his nervous system causes him to suffer more anguish than many who are physically ill. He is never really ill, yet never really well, and his deplorable condition renders him a misery to himself and to everybody with whom he comes into contact. He eats badly, sleeps badly, thinks badly, works badly, plays badly – does everything badly – in fact he is more dead than alive! He worries incessantly over all manner of trivial things which a healthy-minded person would laugh at ; he broods over imaginary fears and illnesses and convinces himself that he suffers from any complaint that happens to be "poplar," – at the slightest suggestion of any disease becoming an epidemic he is quite sure that he has "got it." He always looks on the black side of everything and insists upon meeting trouble more than half way, in fact, he does not seem to be satisfied until he has reduced himself to the state of a complete nervous wreck.

His visits to his private doctor are so frequent that

the latter secretly regards him as a nuisance and becomes tired of repeatedly telling his sceptical patient that there is nothing organically wrong with him and that he must "pull himself together" – advice which usually falls on deaf ears because the neurasthenic usually convinces himself that he is suffering from some terrible malady which the doctor is hiding from him for fear of giving him a shock which might prove fatal! Losing faith in his doctor, he then doses himself with every patent medicine and quack remedy on the market and wonders why he gets worse instead of better.

If the above little pen-picture fits you, dear reader, please do not think I wish to make fun of your condition; I only wish to show you the folly of letting your imagination run away with you, and I am sure you will have a very different outlook when you have read this Course.

NERVOUS FEARS ARE OF YOUR OWN CREATION. I am of the opinion that all nervous fears and disorders having a purely mental origin are absolutely created by the sufferer himself.

All forms of fear are induced in the same way. If you are afraid of thunderstorms; if you are nervous of crossing a busy road; if you fell oppressed and stifled in a closed room; if you dread being alone (or, on the otherhand, being in a crowd); if you fear illness or failure; if you sleep badly; if you are terrified of death, or dread "the end of the world"; if you have suicidal tendencies or a fear of becoming insane; if you are subject to attacks of depression, worry and morbid thoughts; if you have a horror of harmless creatures such as spiders, mice, etc. – in short, whatever "pet fear" you may be the victim of, I want you to realise that your weakness is self-induced and caused by your own mis-directed thoughts.

Not only are these nervous fears caused by the sufferer himself but they are intensified by the habit of concentrating attention upon them. The more you think about your nervousness (in the wrong light) the more nervous will you become. Consciously or unconsciously, you are always allowing your nervous weakness to dwell upon your mind; you are constantly reminding yourself that you are nervous, and you have allowed this idea to prey upon your mind to such an extent that your nervous fear has become a definite part of your personality. As soon as you have learned how to change the direction of your thoughts, as you will be instructed to do later on, you will find it quite easy to banish your nervousness and develop a bold, fearless and confident personality instead.

I want to explain this point a little more fully in order to convince you that your nervous fears – whatever form they may take – are brought on entirely by yourself. When once you fully appreciate this vital fact your cure will be a simple matter.

HOW NERVOUSNESS IS SELF-INDUCED. In order that we may arrive at a clearer understanding of the psychology of fear, and to prove definitely and conclusively the very important point that fear is self-induced, let us carefully analyse the sensations created within the mind of a person whilst under the influence of fear.

We will take the form of self-fear known as Self-consciousness first. If you are afflicted with Self-consciousness you have an intense dread of associating with strangers, or even friends and relatives. You have a horror of entering strange company; of being introduced to people, especially those of the opposite sex; you dread having to stand out of the crowd as someone of particular interest – you loathe being dragged into the limelight. You hate publicity, shun leadership and object to being thanked, praised or complimented. Wherever you may be you are always under the impression that everyone is watching you and making fun of your embarrassment. You believe yourself to be an object of ridicule and humorous attraction everywhere. Except when in the privacy of your own home, you are always uncomfortable and ill-at-ease; your mind is seldom calm and composed. If you have a tendency to pity yourself – an unfortunate failing of most self-conscious people – this intensifies your animosity towards those who fail to understand and sympathise with you and probably compels you to adopt a retiring and hermit-like existence, enjoying little more social intercourse than a recluse.

Because you have an abject terror of meeting and conversing with your fellow-men, or of entering company, or of appearing in the limelight, you do your utmost to avoid these things by refusing invitations (which you would really be delighted to accept); by failing to "answer back" in an argument (even when you know you are right), and by keeping within your shell of reserve as much as possible. Thus you pander to your weakness and encourage its development by admitting its presence and by mentally affirming to yourself on every possible occasion, "I can't, because I am too shy!"

So, you see, you are actually (though perhaps unconsciously) forcing yourself to be nervous by allowing your mind to continually dwell upon your complaint, and by deliberately expecting and firmly believing that you will be nervous on certain occasions because you usually are!

To take another example, suppose you are afraid of thunderstorms; what do you do when a storm approaches? At the first distant rumble of thunder you immediately remind yourself that you are afraid of storms, and you then commence to re-create within your mind the same sensation of fear and oppression that you always experience during a thunderstorm. You do this automatically and you convince yourself, even before the storm arrives, that you will again be afraid because you always are. Remember, you induce this fear absolutely yourself; you know that other people around you are not afraid, although they are exposed to the same "danger" as yourself, yet you work yourself into a frenzy of terror and apprehension while other persons near you are quite calm and unafraid.

Although you have seen hundreds of thunderstorms and have always come through unharmed, you convince yourself every time that you may be struck by lightning, and yet storms come and go and nothing untoward ever happens to you! You probably never feel afraid of being killed while crossing a road, but you expect to be killed every time a thunderstorm arises. Actually your chances of being killed while crossing a road are a thousand time greater than the chances of being killed by lightning, for statistics show that although thousands of people are killed in road accidents every year, only one person in a million is killed by lightning! The mere fact that other people placed under the same conditions are not afraid of storms is convincing proof that the few who are afraid must induce this fear themselves.

Just one more illustration to prove that all forms of fear are self-induced and due entirely to the perverted imagination of the sufferer. This time we will take sleeplessness – not exactly a "fear," but a nervous disorder that, like so many others, is created and intensified by the sufferer himself. Why do you fail to drop off to sleep quickly when you go to bed, or lie awake – for hours after a short early sleep? For the simple reason that you retire every night with the firm conviction that you will have "a bad night" – because you usually do! The belief that you will again get little sleep is uppermost in your mind when you retire, and it is not to be wondered at that after making up your mind that you will sleep badly that you do sleep badly.

This habit of convincing yourself that you will be nervous, or that your nervous disorder will manifest itself, simply because it is a customary phase of your temperament, is characteristic of almost every type of neurasthenic disorder and this is really the primary cause of all forms of nerve-weakness.

ALL NERVOUS FEARS HAVE THE SAME CAUSE. Although I have given only three examples of self-induced fear, I want you to understand that what I have written applies to all other forms of nerve-weakness having a purely mental basis. Obviously, it is not possible for me to deal with every one of the hundreds of types of nervous disorders in existence, and I have given these three examples as typical of the type of nervous ailments which are self-induced. The foregoing remarks, therefore, equally apply to all the forms of nervous and mental afflictions that this Course is designed to cure, and, obviously, the treatment prescribed for one form of nervousness will be equally beneficial to all.

I particularly want you to realise that the combination of circumstances which causes a person to be nervous in one direction also causes another person to be nervous in another direction. For instance, one person may be afraid of lightning; another person may not care a rap about storms and yet be terrified of being alone in the dark, whilst another person may laugh at both of these fears and yet shriek at the sight of a mouse! All these fears and phobias – and there are hundreds of them – have the same underlying cause, and as the cause is the same the cure must be the same also.

WHAT IS THE CAUSE OF NERVOUSNESS? What is the dominating influence that exercises so powerful a hold over our personalities and causes us to think and act contrary to our desires? Why are some people so terrified of certain things whilst others fear nothing and nobody? Briefly, the underlying cause of all the nervous disorders dealt with in this Course is:

The Lack of Complete Control of our Emotions and a Deficiency of Will-Power.

The sole reason why you feel nervous, depressed or worried under certain circumstances is simply because your will not strong enough to prevent it. You have allowed what little will-power you once possessed to run so low that you have not sufficient energy left "to pull yourself together" and ward off the undesirable impulses that cause you to feel nervous. Therefore, it is obvious that by strengthening your will-power all these groundless fears, imaginary complaints and self-induced ailments can be cured.

In the following sentence you have the whole teaching of this Course in six words!

The Development of Will-Power KILLS Nervousness!

I hope you understand the significance of that statement. It is important that you should realise that the real solution of all your troubles depends upon the development of a strong will. You are nervous only because you lack sufficient will-power to be courageous. When you feel the dreaded sensation of fear coming over you, you are absolutely helpless; you are so weak-willed that you are quite powerless to

27

check your emotion, and, losing all control of yourself, you are forced to submit to the dominating power of your disordered mind, allowing your fears to completely master you. If only you could get your will under complete control it would be a simple matter to master your nerves. This may not seem quite clear to you yet, but you will understand this better when you have read the two following Parts of this Course.

In concluding this Part, I will give you a sentence which sums up the whole of my teaching so far:

Your Nervous Fears are Caused by Your Inability to Control Impulses that certain Suggestions Convey to Your Mind.

Every time you encounter a fear-provoking situation a suggestion, or command, to be nervous is conveyed to your brain, and because you have not sufficient will-power to reject it, your brain obeys the command and you immediately become nervous. I am afraid this may sound rather vague, but the action of the mind of the nerve sufferer rightly belongs to the next Part, in which it will be fully explained.

PART 2

MODERN PSYCHOTHERAPY

LESSON 1

The Theory of Suggestion

In the preceding part of this Course I have endeavoured to explain to you just what nervous disorders are and why you are nervous, and I hope I have given you a clearer insight into your own particular nerve trouble than you have ever had before. We now have to consider the best means of curing your nervousness and I think you will readily agree that medicine is definitely ruled out as useless and that we shall have to resort to something more effective than drugs.

I have previously stated that in order to cure yourself it is only necessary to get your emotions completely under your control, and to do this you must increase your will-power. How can this be accomplished? The most efficient method of developing the will is by means of Psychotherapy, the modern method of scientific mental treatment. Psychotherapy is the medical term for what is better known as Curative Suggestion. In various forms it is used in hospitals and mental institutions and by nerve-specialists and doctors all over the world.

Now, before proceeding further, I must tell you that in writing this section of my Course I shall presume that I am addressing a person who knows absolutely nothing about psychotherapeutic treatment, and I must ask those of my readers who are not entirely unacquainted with the subject to excuse my elementary explanations and the general simplicity of the whole Course. For the benefit of any of my readers who may have "dabbled" in this form of treatment before without success, let me assure you at once that you will find my methods quite unlike the usual style of suggestive treatment, and I may add that a considerable number of my patients who had previously tried this form of curative treatment without result, have had no difficulty in curing themselves under this Course. I shall endeavour to put the subject before you in such a way as will, I am sure, thoroughly convince you, not only that this wonderful natural power is all that it is claimed to be, but also that with its aid all your nervous fears and disorders can be completely eradicated.

WHAT SUGGESTION IS. I now propose to explain to you as simply as possible exactly what Curative Suggestion is and how it operates. First of all, I ask you not to be too ready to disbelieve in the power which I am about to describe to you, but to suspend your judgment until you have read this Course to the end. It is not only unfair but also rather foolish to condemn anything one does not thoroughly understand.

A great deal of nonsense has been written about Suggestion, especially in America, and several enterprising cranks have tried to create the impression that Suggestion is some inexplicable spiritual gift accessible only to believers who possess some sort of "faith," whereas it is a perfectly natural power possessed by every human being. Let me at once assure you that there is nothing weird, mysterious nor supernatural about Suggestion. Stripped of its technical phraseology and the highbrow nonsense with which so many writers have associated it, we shall see that Suggestion, although a truly wonderful force, is not at all the mysterious phenomena that it is often made out to be.

What, then, is Suggestion? Dr. Bernheim of the famous Nancy School of France, who was probably the first physician to put suggestive treatment on a practical working basis, describes Suggestion as, "The aptitude of the brain to receive or evoke ideas, and its tendency to realise them and to transform them into acts." Dr. Bernard Hollander, the eminent nerve-specialist, uses the expression, "A process of communication of an idea to the subconscious mind." My own definition of Suggestion is:

A Voluntary, or Involuntary, Actuating Impulse by Means of which every Thought or Idea is Transformed into Action.

Or, to put the matter into simple language, we might describe Suggestion as the motive power behind our thoughts and actions – the invisible something which prompts us every time we think, say or do anything.

In my opinion, Suggestion is a kind of sixth sense – a natural power already within our consciousness, and not, as some psychologists assert, something that has to be acquired or cultivated. Every man, woman and child has the suggestive ability dormant within them, ready to be brought into use when required. Suggestion must not be confused with its predecessor, Hypnotism, which can only be acquired and responded to by certain individuals, whereas Suggestions can be, and is, used by everybody.

What is claimed for Curative Suggestion is this: that by earnestly and persistently "suggesting" to ourselves that the complaint from which we are suffering does not exist, we can completely cure the disorder! This sounds rather incredible, does it not? But when you understand the object of telling yourself that you are not ill and how that statement reacts on your mind, you will see that this is not so absurd as it may at first appear. It may seem absurd to say, "I am not nervous," when you know perfectly well that you are nervous, but this obviously untruthful statement has a definite object, and that object is to influence the impressionable subconscious mind to such an extent that it eventually accepts the statement as true! I am aware that all this sounds rather vague, but my meaning will be perfectly clear to you when you have read the whole of this Course.

VARIOUS FORMS OF SUGGESTION. There are several forms of Suggestion, and in order that you may easily follow my remarks I had better explain them before we go any further. In this Course I shall deal with three kinds of Suggestion and I shall call them Involuntary-Suggestion, Counter-Suggestion and Auto-Suggestion.

Involuntary-Suggestion operates subconsciously, that is, without any effort on our part, and often without our being aware of the fact. It was Involuntary-Suggestion to which I referred previously as being the "invisible something" which prompts us every time we think, speak or act. The action of Involuntary-Suggestion is controlled by the subconscious mind – that section of the brain which causes the heart to beat, the lungs to breathe, the stomach to digest and the various other organs to perform their respective functions without any conscious effort on the part of the individual.

Counter-Suggestion is that which is used consciously and voluntarily, either by ourselves or others, with the object of counteracting or breaking down undesirable involuntary suggestions. Auto-Suggestion (or Self-Suggestion), as the term implies, is that which is administered entirely by the sufferer himself.

The type of Suggestion which, as I shall explain later, is responsible for your nervous conditions is Involuntary-Suggestion, and that which we shall employ to cure you will be a combination of Counter-Suggestion and Auto-Suggestion.

YOU USE SUGGESTION EVERY DAY. I want you to realise that every one of us regularly uses Involuntary-Suggestion in our daily lives. Although you have probably been totally ignorant of the fact until now, you are continually giving yourself Suggestion not only every day but almost every minute. For instance, every time you eat or drink you are actuated by the suggestions of hunger or thirst; when you cry you do so in response to a suggestion of sorrow; when you laugh you are moved by a suggestion of joy; and when you sleep you are responding to a suggestion of fatigue. In fact, everything you do must originate from a self-administered suggestion. The following example will illustrate my meaning. After waking up in the morning you may lie in a semi-drowsy state for a few minutes with the thought running through your mind, "I must not lie in bed, I'll get up now." Then your thoughts turn to something else and your resolution to get up is temporarily forgotten. A few moments later you suddenly find yourself getting out of bed, although you hardly realised that you had moved. You are so used to this that you take no notice of it, but if you stop to consider the thought which prompted the action you will realise that it was Suggestion which aroused you. When you said, "I'll get up now," you sent a suggestion to your nerve-centre and although your conscious mind forgot it, your subconscious mind remembered to put the suggestion into operation.

I could give dozens of similar instances of suggestions which we use every day, but you will probably be able to recall them yourself. Although you have probably never stopped to think about it before, I hope you now realise that everything we think, say or do is the result of suggestions we give ourselves.

NERVOUS COMPLAINTS CAUSED BY SUGGESTION. Suggestion is both the cause and the cure of nervous complaints! It will probably surprise you to learn (although you ought to have guessed as much already) that your nervousness is entirely caused by Suggestion. If you stop to consider your case for a moment you will have to admit that you are constantly allowing your thoughts to dominate you and to induce you to feel nervous. For instance, if you are afraid of thunderstorms your thoughts (or, rather suggestions) run in this way, "I do hope we are not going to have a storm, I'm so terrified of lightning!" If you are afraid of traffic you often repeat the suggestion, "I am scared to death of crossing a road." If you fear insanity, your constant thought is, "I am sure I shall eventually go mad!" When you feel depressed or unwell you say to yourself, "I am so miserable, I do feel ill." If your fear is that you are doomed to failure you are constantly telling yourself, "I know I shall never succeed." If you are self-conscious you are always thinking, "I am terribly shy." Since all these thoughts are powerful suggestions, can you wonder at them influencing you as they do?

From whatever nervous complaint you suffer, or whatever form our fears may take, you are giving yourself these injurious suggestions every day. Every time you feel nervous, afraid, depressed or worried, you are reacting to a self-administered suggestion. Every moment of your life your complaint is always on your mind. Everywhere and at all times that dread spectre haunts you; you feel that you cannot banish it from your mind for an instant, and you live in constant dread that something will happen to bring your weakness into prominence and make you nervous. In fact, so great a hold over you has your obsession obtained that it has become a part of yourself – a blemish in your personality that you feel you can never shake off. I hope you now realise that this continual worrying, this anxiety, this horror of becoming nervous, ill or afraid is entirely due to Self-Suggestion.

If these purely involuntary suggestions of fear can have such a marked effect upon you, how much more powerful would be the effect of suggestions of an opposite nature when voluntarily and deliberately administered!

Therefore, in order to conquer your nervous fears of to cure your mental affliction, it is only necessary to give yourself stronger suggestions of calmness, composure boldness and confidence to overpower the involuntary suggestions of nervousness which you have been unconsciously giving yourself in the manner explained. As voluntary Suggestion is naturally much more powerful than involuntary Suggestion, by using the former you kill the weaker suggestions and so destroy the impulse that makes you nervous.

SUGGESTION HAS ALMOST LIMITLESS POSSIBILITIES. There is practically no limit to the uses to which Suggestion can be put, for it must not be supposed that this wonderful subconscious gift of nature is only applicable to ill-health. A bad habit, a poor memory, an imaginary grievance, indecision, laziness – all such weaknesses of character can be corrected by properly applied Suggestion. There is hardly a complaint which cannot be benefited to some extent by Suggestion, although it will be understood that only disorders of a purely mental origin can actually be cured by Suggestion. It must not be imagined that Suggestion can perform miracles – although some of the cures achieved by this means might almost be termed miraculous – for it is only efficacious in disorders where actual disease does not exist. To attempt to cure appendicitis, for instance, by Suggestion would be absurd, for here bodily disease is present and nothing but the surgeon's knife can remove it. It is in cases where the disorder exists principally in the sufferer's mind that Suggestion is of the greatest benefit, and the disorders enumerated in this Course, being purely mental afflictions, are particularly suitable for suggestive treatment.

Suggestion is an omnipresent ability, power or impulse, a natural phase of the mind of every sane individual, which can be regulated or controlled as desire when properly understood. As distinct from Hypnotism, which is introduced from outside and cannot be influenced by ourselves, Suggestion is a power already within us and is continually at work as long as we live.

SUGGESTION IS THE OLDEST REMEDY IN THE WORLD. Although it is only of comparatively recent years that Suggestion has been put into extensive use for the cure of nervous disorders, yet there is nothing new in this method of treatment. In some form or other it has been practised since the world began; indeed, I maintain that life would be impossible without it.

LESSON II

The Working of the Nervous System

Without boring you by entering upon a long discussion of the intricate working of the brain and nervous system, I want to explain a little of the mechanism of the mind in order that you will understand how Suggestion works. You are probably aware that every thought we think, every word we utter and every action we perform is originated in the brain. The analysis of the translation of a mental sensation into physical action will make this clear. Let us suppose that in the act of sharpening a pencil I suddenly cut my finger. The pain comes so quickly that I appear to feel it the instant the knife cuts the skin, but this is not so. At the precise moment when the sharp blade came into contact with the delicate nerve-fibres of my skin a message was flashed along the nerves to my brain, and from there the message was transmitted through another set of nerves back to the cut in my finger, and then – and not till then – I felt pain.

All our thoughts and actions follow the same procedure and we can neither think, say nor do anything until the message has first passed through the brain. We cannot lift an eyelid nor move a finger without the brain being first brought into action, but of course our thoughts operate so quickly that we are quite unconscious of the work being carried out.

THE SENSORY AND MOTOR NERVES. Briefly, there are two sets of nerves employed in executing our desires and carrying out our thoughts and actions. They are the sensory nerves which carry messages to the brain, and the motor nerves which relay the messages

39

from the brain. Reverting to the illustration of my cut finger, the sensory nerves carried the message to the brain that the cut had been made, and then the motor nerves flashed the message back to the wound and operated the sensitive nerves in my finger, so that the pain was felt.

HOW SUGGESTION OPERAT|ES. The sensory nerves are employed in carrying suggestions to the brain and the motor nerves see that the suggestions are carried out. If my head ached and I wished to cure it by Suggestion I should suggest to myself, "My head does not ache." The sensory nerves would carry the suggestion to the nerve-centre and the motor nerves would extend the message to the seat of the pain, and, by translating thought into action, the cause would be removed and the pain banished. Needless to say, Suggestion does not operate quite so quickly and easily as this, but it works in this manner.

I hope it is now quite clear to you that to effect a cure by means of Suggestion the idea is to repeatedly "suggest" to our minds that the disorder does not exist. Every time we give ourselves a suggestion the sensory nerves faithfully carry the message to the nerve-centre, but it is not always easy to arouse the motor nerves into action. That is the reason why it is necessary to repeat the suggestion several times, but if we persevere and continue to utter the suggestion with patience and determination, the motor nerves must obey our commands in due course.

THE TELEPHONE OF THE BRAIN. To adopt a very simple means of explaining the working of the brain and nervous system we may compare them with a telephone installation. For the purpose of this illustration we require only two lines and a central exchange. The line which accepts the message, that is, the wire from our house to the exchange, may be compared with the sensory nerves which receive all messages to be communicated to the centre of the nervous system. The line which relays the message to the desired destination, that is, the wire from the exchange to the place with which we wish to communicate, is represented by the motor nerves, and the exchange is represented by the centre of the nervous system. In order to carry out any desired act we first send the thought or message to the exchange (nerve-centre) via the sensory nerves, and from there it is transmitted by the motor nerves to the various nerves and muscles required to perform the desired act.

Now let us see what happens when you give yourself the suggestion that you are not nervous. When you say, "I am not nervous," you are speaking into the transmitter of the sensory nerves, so to speak. The message reaches the exchange alright, but here your message may not be properly understood (your suggestions is not yet effective), and the exchange operator does not make the connection. You call again, giving your message plainer (strengthening the suggestion). Still no action. You speak plainer and more determined still (make the suggestion even stronger). This time you are understood and the desired connection is made (the motor nerves are set in motion causing your suggestion to be carried into effect).

This simple telephone illustration explains the operation of Suggestion better, perhaps, than pages of technical description and physiological diagrams.

DISORDERED NERVES ARE NOT DISEASED. Many nerve-specialists are of the opinion, and I agree with them, that in neurasthenic disorder the wires of the nervous system (the sensory and motor nerves) may be, and usually are, in perfect order; it is only the exchange (the nerve-centre) that is at fault. In your present state the sensory nerves are quite capable of carrying messages to the central department and the motor nerves are competent to translate them into actions, but the central department itself is in a state of chaos, it is so badly disorganised that it has no power to eliminate undesirable suggestions, and so all manner of impulses that tend to increase your nervousness are allowed to get through and play havoc with your nervous system. To put a stop to all this and to restore yours nerves to a state of calmness and composure, the first step is to get your nerve-centre under control and then to administer suggestions of a nature that will destroy the undesirable suggestions that have for so long held such sway over your mental personality.

AUTOMATIC NERVOUS MANIFESTATIONS. The sensory and motor nerves of a nervous person have merely become disorganised, the central station has lost its control over them. Through force of habit the combined working of the sensory and motor nerves causes you to feel nervous, depressed or afraid on the slightest provocation. Let me illustrate this. Supposing you are afraid of thunderstorms, immediately a storm approaches your fear instantly manifest itself. From habit or instinct you know that you will feel terrified, but although you do your utmost to control yourself, you are quite powerless to prevent your customary fear from asserting itself. Why?

Simply because this Fear has become so Firmly Fixed in your Consciousness that whenever a Storm arises the Sensation of Fear is Aroused quite Automatically!

In other words, the motor nerves set the "fear of storms" mechanism in action without even waiting for instructions. (Like a horse that regularly stops at its destination through force of habit without waiting to be pulled up by the driver).

CONSTANT REPETITION CREATES A FIXED IDEA. In the case of a nervous person we may say that the most prominent idea within his mind is the knowledge that he is nervous. His condition is so often on his mind and his nervousness so frequently manifests itself that it requires little or no effort to bring it into prominence. In fact, the sensory nerves have become so used to calling up his nervous condition that it can accomplish this task easier and quicker than any other. He has so often given himself the suggestion, "I am nervous," that the constant repetition has created a fixed idea in his mind that he must be nervous on every possible occasion. The operation of what may, for the sake of simplicity, be termed the fear impulse has thus become purely mechanical and automatic, and the nervous person finds that it is as easy to feel nervous as it is to write his name.

It is evident that to put a stop to this involuntary arousing of the fear impulse we must first eradicate from the mind the idea, or suggestion, that is responsible for its manifestation. When we contemplate the complex formation of the brain and its automatic manner of working this seems an impossible feat, and, before the advent of psychotherapeutic treatment, it certainly was; but it is here that Suggestion proves it inestimable value, for with its aid the mind can be regulated and controlled almost as desired.

CONSCIOUS AND SUBCONSCIOUS MIND. The human mind, elementarily speaking, is divided into two parts – the conscious mind and the subconscious mind. The conscious mind, obviously, operates with our knowledge and is, to a certain extent, under our control, but the subconscious mind operates automatically without any effort on the part of the individual. Before we can repeat anything that we have thought, said or done before, that is, before we can produce an idea from the subconscious mind, it must first be transferred to the conscious mind, when it becomes known to us. I will try to explain this. When you hear a certain song being sung, before you can recognise it the memory of the previous rendering of the same song must first leave the subconscious mind and enter the conscious mind. Again, when you meet an acquaintance before you can realise that the person is known to you, this fact must first be transferred from the subconscious to the conscious mind.

To illustrate this better, let us analyse the sensations caused by, say, a dish of pineapple. The placing of this object before you excites three senses, sight, taste and smell. You have seen pineapple before, you have tasted it and you have smelt it. Therefore, the records of the sight, taste and smell of pineapple are stored somewhere within the millions of memory cells of the subconscious mind. The instant the pineapple is placed before you the memory of the previous sight of this object is transferred from the subconscious to the conscious memory, when it becomes known to you, or, in other words, you recognise the object as something you have seen before. The senses of taste and smell are aroused in exactly the same manner, but the miraculous speed with which this work of the mind is carried out makes everything appear to us to be instantaneous, as, indeed, it is.

This changing of ideas from the subconscious to the conscious mind and back again never for an instant ceases so long as we retain consciousness. Before we can walk, run, sit, stand, eat, drink, think, speak, feel nervous – in fact, before we can do anything, the subconscious mind must first be brought into use to give us the knowledge and power to perform these acts.

MENTAL STORAGE CELLS. Everything we think, say or do, every task we have ever accomplished, every little incident of our past lives is permanently stored within the limitless cells of the subconscious mind. Opinion on this subject is very diversified and no definite information of the actual mechanism of these wonderful storage cells is yet known. Some students of mental science are of the opinion that in time the memory cells become overcrowded and some of the least important ideas have to be expelled; others (myself included) believe that no idea, however insignificant, is ever lost sight of by the subconscious mind. It is true that the subconscious mind may never again recall thousands of minor incidents, but they are there all the same ready for use should occasion arise.

This manner of retaining thousands of even unimportant ideas is truly amazing, but it must be ranked among the problems which defy elucidation, for scientists are compelled to admit that they can explain neither the mechanism of the action nor the manner in which so many thousands of ideas are stored.

When visiting the theatre or opera you may become enraptured over the strains of an enchanting piece of music, not a note of which you can remember an hour later, but on a future occasion the whole composition may suddenly return to you without effort – thus proving that the memory was there, although you could not recall it when you wished to. The peculiar mental freak of having a very familiar name "on the tip of the tongue" which refuses to reveal itself to you even after considerable mental effort, is a good illustration of the existence of conscious and subconscious memory. This difficulty of recalling a name, even though it is on the tip of your tongue, is due to a temporary disorganisation of the line of communication between the conscious and subconscious mind. The name is in the subconscious mind alright, but the motor nerves refuse to function and so the conscious mind cannot produce the required information. As soon as the line is cleared, or as soon as the mechanism of the mind readjusts itself, the elusive name instantly returns.

What causes those babyish rhymes and melodies that we were taught when children, and which we have forgotten long ago, to return to our minds without cause or reason years later? In what manner do those insignificant incidents enacted many years ago and long since forgotten return again years afterwards with all the vividness and minuteness of detail of their original occurrence?

In attempting to arrive at a solution of this fascinating and truly wonderful problem, we can only conjecture that in some manner as yet unknown to us these ideas and incidents are stored within the limitless cells of the subconscious mind, but in what manner they are stored, or by what process they are transferred to the conscious mind is still a mystery to us. Whether it will ever be solved or whether it really lies beyond the province of human comprehension time alone can prove.

LESSON III

The Method of Applying Auto-Suggestion

The most direct method of applying Auto-Suggestion is by persistently asserting, at regular and suitable periods, that your complaint no long exists. The suggestions to be used for this purpose are voluntary verbal ones; the suggestions which, as I have already explained, cause your nervousness are involuntary mental ones. It is therefore evident that the stronger verbal suggestions, when correctly applied, should have little difficulty in overpowering the weaker mental suggestions. Your object, then, must be to destroy the involuntary suggestions of nervousness by giving yourself voluntary suggestions of courage and confidence.

The correct procedure in employing Auto-Suggestion is to repeat a number of specially prepared sentences (or suggestions) at regular periods and under suitable conditions. A table, or formula, consisting of a few appropriate phrases, in which the existence of the complaint is resolutely denied or referred to as being a thing of the past, should be earnestly and sincerely repeated in private once or twice a day.

At the end of this Course, in Part 3, will be found a number of Suggestion tables which have been carefully prepared to apply to each of the complaints treated. The tables are printed in a clear bold type to facilitate easy reading, and each table is printed on a separate page to enable the user to concentrate his entire attention upon the actual words to be repeated. It is advisable to tear out each table as required, as a separate sheet is more convenient to use than a bulky book. The page containing the table you wish to use should be extracted from the book and placed against any convenient support at a distance from which it can be easily read.

THE STATE OF REPOSE. Many practitioners of psychotherapy advise that a state of semi-consciousness should be induced before administering Suggestion. It is recommended that the patient retires to a room where he is safe from interruption and to lie on a bed or couch in a comfortable position, and then to imitate the sensation of falling asleep until a condition of semi-consciousness (not actual sleep) is reached, when the appropriate suggestions are administered.

It is not always an easy matter to induce this state of semi-coma, and in my opinion such a condition is not at all essential. It must not be supposed, however, that no concentration is necessary, but I have found that a lighter stage of repose is usually quite sufficient for most patients. In deep hypnotism the most profound sleep is absolutely essential; in Auto-Suggestion only the merest drowsiness is said to be necessary, but I go a step further and claim that Suggestion can be successfully used even without the induction of a state of semi-sleep. Indeed, I think I may safely assert that it is quite possible to make effective use of Suggestion without even attempting to induce this condition of partial coma, and I know that many hundreds of my patients have succeeded in curing themselves, although they were unable to acquire very deep concentration.

So do not worry if you are unable to create this condition before practising Suggestion, but I advise you to endeavour to acquire as deep a concentration as you can as the more perfect the repose the more rapid will be the effect of the suggestions.

The purpose of inducing, or trying to induce, this condition of rest and relaxation is to make your mind as blank as possible because the brain is more liable to respond to the suggestions given to it when it is in a calm and peaceful state. The pitch of the voice plays an important part in the repetition of the suggestions. Naturally it would not do to speak in a loud voice while in a state of deep concentration, and it is therefore proper to commence in the merest whisper, increasing the volume of sound as you proceed.

Not only must the voice be increased in volume, but also in enthusiasm. As you approach the final passages of the Suggestion table you should endeavour to feel more and more elated so that by the time you finish the table you are thrilled with enthusiasm at the prospect of soon being cured.

The different degrees of tone employed in repeating the suggestions are arranged in four stages as follows: mentally, in a whisper, softly and aloud. So that each tone may make an equal impression, the softer tones should be repeated more often than the louder tones, as directed in the left-hand margin of each table. The reason for this graduation of tone is that when in the state of repose the suggestions must first enter the consciousness stealthily, gradually becoming more forcible until the last sentence is uttered aloud. In this manner the patient is aroused from his deep concentration in easy stages, until by the time the last and loudest sentence is spoken he is fully awake.

MENTAL ATTITUDE DURING SUGGESTION. The mental attitude of the patient while using Suggestion greatly influences its speed of operation. You must not merely say, "I am not nervous," but you must actually believe it. You see, the idea of making these contradictory suggestions is to put you in the condition you are striving to acquire. You are striving to become a bold, happy and fearless person; then you must endeavour to assume a bold, happy and fearless bearing every time you practise Suggestion. Do you see the object of this? If you wished to learn to play the piano you would naturally imitate the actions of an accomplished player. If you wished to learn French, you would imitate the articulations of a Frenchman. Whatever you wished to learn, you would proceed in the same manner, that is, you would imitate or assume the condition you wished to acquire. As you wish to learn to be a fearless and confident person, you must imitate the thoughts and bearing of a fearless and confident person. Every time you use the Suggestion tables you must pretend that you are no longer a nervous person and this pretence will soon become reality. By suggesting that you are a courageous person you will eventually acquire courage, just as by pretending you can play the piano you will eventually find that you can play the piano.

Imitation is the Surest Means of Acquisition – Practise Makes Perfect!

When you suggest that you are no longer nervous, you are actually imitating a person who is not nervous, and it is only necessary to keep up this pretence long enough to acquire the thoughts and bearing of the person you are imitating.

The actual effect of using Suggestion is that for the few minutes you are repeating the suggestion tables you are really no longer nervous. It therefore follows that by repeatedly assuming the condition you wish to acquire, you will soon make such a deep impression on your subconscious mind that the desired condition will cease to be mere make-belief and become a definite reality. In other words, you eventually convince your subconscious mind that you are not nervous, and the effect is to render the subconscious mind powerless to arouse your previous nervous state.

I must impress upon you the importance of believing that you are no longer nervous while you are actually using Suggestion. When you suggest that you are not nervous, say it with conviction as though it is absurd to imagine that you ever were nervous. Above all, after you have said, "I am not nervous," do not let your mind immediately assert, "Of course I know that is untrue, I am just as nervous as ever!" The effect of such a reaction would be to destroy the good suggestion by setting up a bad suggestion, and as long as you maintained this double-suggesting attitude progress would naturally be retarded.

You must also take care to prevent any mechanical note from entering you voice or manner while using Suggestion. A parrot could be taught to say, "Headache gone, headache gone," but no parrot could cure it aching head by Suggestion! Do you see what I mean? It is possible to say one thing but think entirely different, but as long as you believe what you are saying (which a parrot does not) your suggestion must become effective. I need hardly emphasise the necessity of regular and persistent use of the Suggestion tables; to neglect to practise, even for a few days, might easily undo all the good that Suggestion had already done you. So do not miss your daily practice unless illness or some other cause make this unavoidable.

At first your suggestions will beat against the door of your subconscious mind as the waves beat against the rocks, but as the constant dripping of water will wear away the hardest stone ever quarried, so the constant repetition of an idea will in time penetrate the subconscious mind and become a conscious fact.

HOW TO USE SUGGESTION. The correct procedure for the administration of Suggestion will now be explained. Having retired to a private room, or some other place where you are not likely to be disturbed, you should sit or lie down in a comfortable attitude and place the Suggestion table before you. It does not matter what position you assume so long as you are able to rest quietly and comfortably. You may prefer to sit at a desk or table with the Suggestion table lying in front of you, or you may find it more convenient to pin the table to a wall and read it while lying on a bed or couch, or, again, you may prefer to lay face downwards resting on your elbows with your head supported between your hands, and the table lying in front of you.

Having decided upon the most suitable position, close your eyes for a few moments before repeating the suggestions (you may also place a finger in each ear if there is any disturbing noise outside) and endeavour to make your mind a complete blank. Try to reject all outside thoughts and troubles and concentrate your whole attention upon what you are about to do.

When you are satisfied that your mind is as attentive as you can get it, you may proceed to repeat to suggestions. Concentrating every particle of attention upon what you are saying, repeat each sentence carefully and earnestly in the correct tone and order as indicated on the Suggestion table. Pause for a moment after each sentence so that the full meaning of your utterance thoroughly "sinks in" your mind. When you repeat such a sentence as, "All my former depression has quite gone," say it as though you meant it and try to picture yourself as being quite free from depression. Put every ounce of enthusiasm into such a sentence as, "Thank God I am now cured!" and try to believe what you say, for although it may not be true at first, it will eventually become so.

WHEN TO USE SUGGESTION.   Experience has shown that the best time for the administration of

Suggestion is immediately upon awaking in the morning, for at this time the body is refreshed after the night's rest and the brain, having been working at "slow pressure" for several hours, is in the best condition for receiving and carrying out any suggestions made to it. If you find it inconvenient to use Suggestion in bed or that you have no time to spare before going to business in the morning, you should practice in the evening, or if this time is also impracticable you must arrange the time to suit your own convenience and practice whenever you have a few minutes to spare during the day. Although the morning is the best time for Suggestion, the actual period used does not matter so very much so long as you practice every day and at the same time each day if possible.

Should it be inconvenient for you to retire to a private room for the purpose of practising Suggestion, do not let this worry you, for you will probably be able to obtain a few minutes privacy elsewhere. People living in the country who have a difficulty in securing privacy indoors should remember that the woods and fields offer plenty of quiet retreats to which one can retire without fear of being disturbed. Even town dwellers may be able to use quiet nooks in parks and open places if Suggestion cannot be conveniently practised in private at home. In short, although it is advisable to use Suggestion in the morning and under the conditions stated, you need not bind yourself to any hard and fast rules which are not perfectly convenient for you. Adapt Suggestion to your own needs and circumstances and you need not worry if conditions are not absolutely ideal so long as you practice regularly and under the best conditions you can get.

Do not attempt to use Suggestion if there is any risk of your being disturbed while you are thus engaged; the fear of being interrupted would prevent you from acquiring sufficient concentration, and this might render the suggestions ineffective, or, at least their power.

When you have completed the day's practice of Suggestion, it is advisable to dismiss the matter from your mind and not continue to let your thoughts dwell upon the subject. This gives your subconscious mind plenty of time to ponder over your suggestions, so to speak, and it is more likely to respond to the suggestions if it is subjected to an occasional severe reprimand, as it were, than if the attacks were frequent but feeble. It might help you to regard your subconscious mind as a kind of invisible enemy who is bent upon making your life as unbearable as possible, and it is up to you to determine not to let this enemy defeat you. You will thus appreciate that it is more effective to deliver an occasional terrific onslaught in which you exert yourself to the utmost, than to waste your nervous energy by keeping up a continual barrage of feeble attacks. For this reason Suggestion should not be applied more than once a day; except in very severe cases where twice-daily practice may be advantageous, or, on the other hand, where more than one complaint has to be treated at the same time.

It may be thought that if one application of Suggestion can be so beneficial several applications a day might effect a quicker cure, but it must be remembered that one can have too much of a good thing and that familiarity breeds contempt. So any attempt to overdo Suggestion must be avoided as too frequent use would have the effect of lessening its power.

EMERGENCY SUGGESTION. Although you have been advised not to practice Suggestion more than once, or at the most twice a day, there are occasions when you will find it helpful and beneficial to call in the aid of Suggestion to help you over a trying ordeal, as when you are subjected to an attack of your complaint between the periods of using the Suggestion tables. Supposing, for instance, you are afflicted with Self-consciousness and you find yourself suddenly faced with a situation in which you would normally feel embarrassed. In such an event you should repeat mentally one or two encouraging suggestions, declaring that you are quite cool and composed, with the object of giving yourself sufficient confidence to meet the situation. It is particularly on these occasions when your complaint attacks you unexpectedly that you should take great care not to give way to your feelings, and, above all, not to give yourself suggestions of nervousness, as you have been in the habit of doing in the past. Instead of suggesting that you are nervous or that you will give way to your feelings, just give yourself a suggestion of courage and composure before the involuntary suggestion of nervousness and defeat can get a chance to beat you.

If you are afraid of thunderstorms, for example, you must not give way to your fear – which means allowing the involuntary suggestion of fear to operate without resistance – but when you know that a storm is approaching just repeat several reassuring suggestions affirming that you are not afraid and you will surprised how this will allay your fear.

This form of Suggestion I call Emergency Suggestion, and it should be resorted to at any time when the necessity arises. It may be used for any complaint dealt with in this Course, and it will be found remarkably effective in giving you sufficient confidence to gain temporary command over your emotions until the practice of the ordinary Suggestion tables has completed your cure.

HOW TO PREPARE SPECIAL TABLES. Although the Suggestion tables given in this Course cover most cases of general nerve-weakness, you may find that your particular case may call for slightly different treatment or that the complaint from which you suffer may not be fully represented in the tables I have prepared. If this is the case you will find it quite a simple matter to prepare a special table to meet your personal requirements. It may only be necessary to alter a word here and there in the printed tables, but if you prefer to write out an entirely fresh table the following hints will assist you.

By carefully studying the printed tables you will grasp the idea of their preparation, and, by substituting phrases to suit your complaint, you will not find it very difficult to arrange a table which exactly fits your case. It is most important to remember in writing out special tables that you must never on any account express the hope that you may be cured, but always assert firmly and decisively that you are cured now. The sentences should be written in a simple, natural style, employing just such expressions as you are accustomed to use in your ordinary conversation. Write just as you speak, not as though you were composing an essay, for the sentences have to be spoken by you and should therefore follow your natural speech.

The tables should be so worded as to inspire confidence in you of your ability to cure yourself every time you use them.

A RETROSPETION. Now, my friend, I hope you quite understand all that I have tried to teach you so far. It would be as well if we took a backward glance over the road we have travelled together in order to make sure that you have grasped all that I have endeavoured to explain to you. There are three important points that I want you to thoroughly understand, and they are: (1) the reason why you are nervous, (2) the mental state that has caused your nervous conditions, and (3) the mental state that you must voluntarily create in order to conquer your nervousness. Are all these points clear to you? Do not worry if they are not, for you may find it necessary to read through this Course several times before the full meaning of all that I have told you dawns upon you. The claims of psychotherapeutic treatment are so startling to the learner that it is not always easy to grasp its full meaning at first.

The summary of all that I have written so far is this:

(1) That your nervous condition is merely the manifestation of a super-sensitive nature and a weak will – the result of unconsciously administered injurious suggestions.

(2) That you are nervous simply because you lack complete control of your emotions, and because you have not sufficient will-power to conquer the impulse that makes you nervous.

(3) That to cure your nervousness you must break down and exterminate the involuntary suggestions responsible for it presence by setting up voluntary suggestions of an opposite nature.

Is that all clear? I want you to try to understand these points before you commence to cure yourself. Once the matter is clear to you, the amazing truth of all that I have told you will come upon you like a joyous revelation and you will be astonished and delighted at the realisation of the straightness of the road that lies before you – the road to FREEDOM FROM

NERVOUSNESS.

PART 3

THE PRACTICAL APPLICATION OF SUGGESTION TO NERVOUS DISORDERS

LESSON 1

How to Use Suggestion in Your Own Case

We now arrive at what is, from your point of view, the most important section of the whole Course. In this last Part of my treatment I shall tell you how to use Suggestion in your case, giving you explicit instructions for completely eradicating your nervous disposition. In Part One I have explained the cause and nature of your nerve-weakness; in Part Two I have described what Suggestion is and how it operates, and now we have to consider how Suggestion is to be employed in order that your will-power can be increased, your emotions brought under your control and your nervousness consequently banished.

In the two preceding books I have done my utmost to convince you that your complaint is purely imaginary; I have tried to show you just how you create your fears yourself, and I hope you now firmly believe that you can banish your complaint as easily as you created it. I feel sure that I have succeeded in convincing you on these two vital points and I sincerely hope you are now fired with an enthusiastic desire to test the wonderful power of Suggestion upon yourself. In a few hours time you will be ready to commence practising Suggestion; in a week or two from now you will be feeling the benefit of your early efforts, and in a month of two (or even sooner) you should be completely free from every trace of nervousness!

In the following pages I shall discuss the various nervous disorders which this Course is designed to cure, giving a few explanatory notes and final words of advice on each of the complaints dealt with. I want you to read very carefully the notes on the particular complaint, or complaints, from which you suffer, and then, when you are ready, to repeat the appropriate Suggestion Table, as directed in Part Two, every morning on rising, or, if more convenient, every evening before retiring.

IMAGINARY FEARS AND DELUSIONS. Under this heading may be grouped all those unreasonable fears, delusions and hallucinations which have no physical basis and which either exist entirely in the sufferer's imagination or else have developed from quite insignificant events by the morbid introspection of the sufferer. Persons afflicted in this way seem to live in constant apprehension of something dreadful happening, or of being stricken with some disease or infirmity, or of some other dire calamity befalling them – and this anticipatory fear causes more worry than the thing itself would do if it ever materialised, which it never does!

The following little parable well illustrates the power of Suggestion in such cases. "Where are you going?" asked a Pilgrim on meeting the Plague one day. "I am going to Baghdad to kill five thousand people," was the reply. A few days later the Pilgrim met the Plague returning. "You told me you were going to kill five thousand people," said the Pilgrim, "but you killed fifty thousand." "No," said the Plague, "I killed five thousand, as I said I would, the others died of fright!"

Far more people die of fright than of actual disease; far more dread something happening to them than ever actually experience the thing dreaded. Just as the extraction of a tooth is never so dreadful as the anticipation of the operation leads one to expect, so the actual materialisation of these imaginary horrors would be far less terrible than we force ourselves to believe beforehand. The greatest troubles in life are those that never happen, so don't count your chickens before they are hatched and don't meet trouble half way. Many a man has "worried himself to death" at the prospect of losing his job, only to find that the expected dismissal never materialised and that he worried himself for nothing. Thousands of people spend years of their lives in utter misery through convincing themselves that they are afflicted with cancer or consumption, or some other fatal disease, which they haven't got and never will have.

If you have read this Course carefully you will now know that all your imaginary fears and hallucinations – no matter what they may be – are all caused by self-suggestion, and that they can be cured by the same means. In Suggestion Table No.1 you will find a real solution of all these worrying groundless fears.

DEPRESSION, WORRY, ANXIETY, ETC. If the cause of your depression or worry is known you must try your utmost to remove it. If you are depressed as a result of some other complaint, such as Self-consciousness, the depression will vanish when you have cured the contributory disorder by means of Suggestion. Do not make mountains out of mole-hills, most of your troubles are greatly exaggerated by dwelling upon them. Do not cry over spilt milk; it is useless worrying over past events which cannot be rectified. However bad your trouble may seem, you may be sure that plenty of other people are worse off than you are, and you should try to derive consolation from the thought that, black as your troubles may seem to be, they might have been much worse than they are.

Think of the many times during your past life when you have been just as worried, depressed or anxious as you are now. Enormous as these troubles seemed at the time, they seem quite insignificant now, do they not? In a few weeks time your present worries will seem just as insignificant as the troubles of the past seem to-day, and as you got over your past troubles so you can just as surely surmount your present difficulties. Forget the present and think only of the future; look ahead to the happy time when you will be able to laugh at your present worries, just as you can now laugh at the troubles of years ago. In the past you have had to conquer your difficulties without the aid of Suggestion, but now that you have this wonderful power to help you, how much easier it will be to overcome your present and future troubles!

Use Suggestion Table No. 2 (and any others that may apply to your case) and you will soon find your present cloud of depression vanishing like smoke in the wind!

THE FEAR OF BECOMING INSANE. I should like to think that only a very small percentage of my patients were in need of advice on overcoming the dread of insanity, but, unfortunately, I know from experience that quite a considerable number of nerve-sufferers secretly dread that they will eventually lose their reason as a result of their nervous disorders The fear of becoming insane is not an uncommon symptom of many forms of neurasthenic ailments, especially where acute depression exists, and it is often manifested after a serious nervous breakdown or prolonged mental distress. The intense depression resulting from many nervous complaints, particularly when they have been endured for several years, often causes the despairing sufferer to imagine that such great mental exhaustion must eventually lead to insanity. Believe me, this is very seldom the case. It is astonishing what the human brain can stand before it will finally break down under the strain of nervous exhaustion, and, considering the enormous number of people who suffer from nervous disorders, the percentage of cases of insanity resulting therefrom is very small indeed.

You will probably be greatly relieved to know that people who fear that they will go insane seldom actually do – those who do lose their reason usually do so without realising it. So you can console yourself with the knowledge that it is practically impossible for you to become insane because you are afraid of insanity, and this fear, strangely enough, will help you to keep your sanity.

Since the possibility of your becoming insane is so very remote, do you not agree that it is foolish to worry about something that will probably never happen? If this dread of going insane is the result of some other nervous disorder, it will only be necessary to apply Suggestion for the cure of the contributory disorder to cause this fear to vanish. I advise you to read my remarks on Depression and Imaginary Fears and Delusions, and, if necessary, you may find it helpful to use the Suggestion Tables for these complaints as well as the special Table No. 3.

DREAD OF SUICIDE. As with those who fear insanity, persons who are afraid that they might commit suicide very rarely get beyond the stage of merely contemplating the act! Suicide always occurs during temporary insanity, and unless you go insane, which, as I have explained in the previous paragraph, is very unlikely, there is very little possibility of your ever taking your life.

The inclination to commit suicide is usually only a temporary weakness, and if only the person afflicted with this morbid tendency would forget the present and think how different his outlook might become a few weeks hence, he would easily overcome the desire to give way under the strain of present difficulties. Many persons who have foolishly committed suicide in a momentary fit of depression would never have been so rash if they had stopped to consider that their depression was merely a temporary phase which would pass off as hundreds of other equally distressing periods had done in the past.

Recall the many trouble and disappointments of your past life and you will admit that they did not last long. Your troubles of to-day are just as fleeting and they will pass off just as they have done before if you will only bear up and let Time, the merciful healer, obliterate your present worries. When once the tragic step has been taken it is too late to change one's mind, and the indescribable horror that many poor souls must have experienced in their last moments of life upon realising, when it was too late to return, that they really wanted to live, is too awful to contemplate.

You may rest assured that however frequently you experience the fear that you will be compelled to take your life, it is very improbable that you will ever do so, so why worry unnecessarily? A few weeks use of Suggestion Table No. 4 will soon drive all such stupid and cowardly ideas from your mind. Read also the paragraphs on Imaginary Fears, Depression and Fear of Becoming Insane.

FEAR OF STORMS. If you have read my remarks on how the fear of storms is induced (see Part One) you will know that your fear of thunder and lightning is absolutely groundless and that there is practically no danger in storms. This knowledge should allay your fears considerably and a short practice of Suggestion Table No. 5, together with the use of an emergency suggestion when a storm arises, will soon make you snap your fingers at the worst of storms.

INSOMNIA. Although sleeplessness is the cause of a great deal of mental distress and physical discomfort, it is probably the easiest to cure of all nervous complaints by means of Suggestion. Indeed, with the aid of Suggestion one can not only induce deep, restful sleep, but it is also possible to cause oneself to wake up at any desired time after a little practice.

Sufferers from insomnia attach far too much importance to their inability to obtain what they consider sufficient sleep. It is a mistake to imagine that everybody must sleep for a fixed number of hours every night, or that one's health will suffer if the usual amount of sleep is not obtained. There is no harm in lying awake for a few hours during the night; the harm comes from worrying about it – not from the lack of sleep. If you wake up after several hours, sleep and find that you cannot "drop off" again, you may be sure that your brain has had all the rest it needs. On such occasions it is far better to get up and make a cup of tea and read a book, or occupy yourself in some other quiet recreation, than to lie in misery trying to force a tireless brain to sleep when it does not need it. Most of us sleep too much, but while we cannot all emulate Edison, who slept only four hours in every twenty-four, it is a good plan for those who spend many wakeful hours in bed to try going to bed a little later, or, better still, getting up a little earlier in the morning.

Suggestion should be administered after retiring every night, as given Suggestion Table No. 6, and should you wake up during the night you will find that an emergency suggestion will soon send you to sleep again. It will be beneficial if you yawn several times and close your eyes drowsily while repeating the suggestions, pretending that you are thoroughly tired out. Do not "count sheep" or carry out any other often recommended mental gymnastics in an attempt to induce sleep, as this sort of nonsense will only stimulate your brain to further action and keep you awake.

Avoid heavy meals late at night as the nervous energy required to aid digestion will prevent your brain from "settling down." For the same reason games requiring considerable mental exertion should not be played, nor any excitement indulged in later than two or three hours before retiring.

SELF-CONSCIOUSNESS. This is perhaps one of the most peculiar and most harmful of all nervous afflictions, yet it is one of the easiest to cure by Suggestion – although I doubt if it could be successfully eradicated by any other means.

The person suffering from Self-consciousness is something of a phenomenon, in that he endures indescribable mental anguish while at the same time often enjoying perfect physical health. Self-consciousness is not a disease, nor even an indication of ill-health, but is rather a combination of several natural characteristics which have become developed and distorted to an abnormal extent. The victim of Self-consciousness has an unfortunate tendency to attach far too much importance to his own thoughts, actions and appearance; not because he is vain, but simply because he is introspective, over-sensitive and over-eager to create a good impression. In other words, he is over-conscious of himself. He mentally criticises his every thought and action and wonders what other people think of him, and, because he is seldom satisfied that he has said or done the right thing, he underestimates his self-importance and develops an "inferiority complex."

If you suffer from this complaint you should bear in mind that you are not inferior to other people and that you create no more attention in a crowd that any other person. You must conquer the mistaken idea that you are being stared at or unflatteringly criticised in public, and you should try to think less of yourself and more of what is going on around you. The only reason why you are different from other people is because, while others do not care a rap what they look like or what other persons think of them, you are always sensitive of these things; forget yourself and your shyness will cease to trouble you.

Imagination is the predominant cause of Self-consciousness: how many times have you noticed that certain dreaded ordeals have proved to be much less embarrassing than you previously forced yourself to believe they would be? A nervous employee may stand trembling outside the terrifying private office of his equally terrifying employer, quaking with fear at the thought of the impending interview, only to find, after eventually plucking up sufficient courage to enter, that he was not half so nervous as he expected to be. Do not try to avoid embarrassing situations but welcome them as opportunities of proving that you are conquering your natural reserve. Get about as much as you possibly can and never refuse an invitation which affords an opportunity of meeting people and improving your conversational abilities. Even if you only walk about the crowded street it will help you to get used to other people and to overcome your natural dislike of company. When you feel inclined to blush, immediately repeat an emergency suggestion such as: "I can face this situation without blushing; now that I am using Suggestion I have complete control of myself and I cannot blush now."

Use Suggestion Table No. 7 regularly every day –

twice daily if your case is very severe – and make emergency suggestions your weapon of defence whenever the necessity arises.

NERVOUS PAINS. As nervous pains, such as headache, neuralgia, neuritis and other neuralgic pains, which may occur in any part of the body, have a physical as well as a mental phase, it is only to be expected that they are rather more difficult to cure than disorders in which no pain is felt, but, as the cause of these physical disturbances is purely mental, they can be completely cured by Suggestion. In the event of such pain being entirely due to some other mental disorder, it will probably cease to attack you when you have cured the disorder which causes it.

If the attacks are fairly frequent, or the complaint of long standing, you should repeat Suggestion Table No. 9 every day whether the pain if present at the time of suggesting or not, and immediately an attack comes on repeat an emergency suggestion to the effect that you have no pain and refuse to believe that any pain exists. I know this is very difficult, but, as you have already learnt, it is owing to the fact that you usually say, "My head aches enough to burst" (or something to that effect), that the pain increases, whereas if you suggest, "My head feels fine, it doesn't ache a bit!" the pain will diminish and eventually vanish altogether.

The Suggestion Table given as an example is for nervous headache, but with a very slight alteration it may be adapted to treat any other nervous pain.

SUPPLEMENTARY SUGGESTION TABLE. After you have used the Suggestion Table applicable to your case for a week or two and you find the Suggestion is definitely making an improvement in your condition, it is sometimes advisable to make a slight change in the method of attack, as it were. So, instead of repeating the same Suggestion Table for the full period of treatment, you may, try a change of formula for the final stage of your cure. Suggestion Table No. 10, which I call the Supplementary Table, has been included for this purpose and it is specially arranged so that it may be used in conjunction with any of the preceding Tables.

Just when this change is to be made depends upon the circumstances of each use, but as soon as you feel that you are deriving benefit from Suggestion you may change over to this Supplementary Table to complete your cure. On the other hand, if you prefer to keep to the one Suggestion Table until you are fully cured you may do so; I have only given this alternate Table for the benefit of those patients who feel that a change of formula would be helpful to them to prevent monotony and to renew their enthusiasm, and, as a general rule, the changing of Tables should only be really necessary in cases where treatment may have to be prolonged.

LESSON II

Concluding Advice

The process of transforming your personality from a nervous and depressed to a bold, fearless and happy one will naturally require a certain amount of patience, especially if your case is very severe, and you must determine to carry on and not give in until you have achieved success. The task before you is a man's job – the man of grit and determination will accomplish it easily enough; only the most abject weakling will admit defeat.

You must not be discouraged if you find that you appear to be as nervous as ever after a few days' practice of Suggestion, nor must you worry if, after making a little progress, you seem to slip back again into your former condition. These set-backs are only temporary, and if you carry on with renewed energy and determination you must win through in the end.

Do not conclude because the effect of the treatment is not early apparent that Suggestion is not doing it work. Suggestion take a little time to get the obstinate subconscious mind under control, but when once this has been accomplished progress towards a complete cure is very rapid. Suggestion operates gradually and stealthily and although you may not notice any marked improvement in your complaint for a week or two, the foundation of your cure is being laid just the same.

My object in mentioning this is merely to prevent you from becoming sceptical and perhaps giving up hope should you find that a few weeks use of the Suggestion Tables makes little noticeable improvement in your condition. Put your whole heart into the persistent practice of the Suggestion Tables and failure will be impossible. To those readers who doubtingly whimper: "It certainly sounds plausible but I doubt if it will do me any good!" I can only earnestly say – put Suggestion to a fair test before condemning it and you will be amazed at what it will do for you.

HOW TO CONQUER PESSIMISM. As a result of his nervous disposition, the sufferer from neurasthenic ailments has an unfortunate tendency to become introspective and to develop a gloomy and pessimistic outlook on life. This is particularly the case with sufferers from Self-consciousness who often shut themselves away from their fellow-creatures, in many cases enjoying little more social intercourse that a recluse. I advise such people to get into the habit of taking a scroll through the busiest street of their town as often as possible. It is surprising how even the mere association of one's fellow-beings in a crowded street or building helps one to forget one's own troubles. Those readers who are afflicted with the fear of storms, for instance, will agree that they do not feel nearly so nervous when they are in a crowded building during a thunderstorm. Loneliness and solitude intensify fear – company and companionship dispel fear.

So, instead of moping alone in the solitude of your home, where you have every opportunity of dwelling upon your troubles, get out into the fresh air, mingle with the throngs of jolly pleasure-seekers and try to acquire some of their jovial, happy-go-lucky spirit of gaiety. Let your visits to theatres, music-halls and other places of entertainment be more frequent. Always look on the sunny side of life, and, like the Jolly Miller in the old song, try to develop an "I care for nobody, no not I, if nobody cares for me" sort of disposition. Don't sit down and wail about your troubles, but set to with a will to conquer them. Above all, do not pity yourself;

feeling sorry for yourself and craving sympathy from those around you is cowardly and demoralising and can only result in your sinking deeper into the mire of despondency. Life is too short to waste in fretting and worrying; go out and enjoy yourself while you can. Look only on the sunny side of everything, take an optimistic view of life and cheer up! Don't imagine that you are the puny, useless little creature that you feel and that your nervousness makes you look, but try to realise that you are a real live animal pulsating with life and energy. Feel proud that you are alive, make people look up to you – not you to them. Don't say, "I can't," say "I WILL!"

HOW TO INCREASE WILL-POWER. I have previously explained that the principal cause of nervous disorders is the lack of sufficient will-power, and that the development of a strong will renders one almost impervious to nerve-trouble. The whole purpose of Suggestion (as far as this Course is concerned) is to increase your will-power, but there are many other ways in which a weak will can be strengthened.

Deficiency of will-power is due not so much to the fact that the ability to possess a strong will is beyond your attainment, as to the fact that you are constantly allowing this vital force to run to waste. For instance, when you decide to have "just another five minutes" after waking in the morning when your usual time of rising is past; when you waste time in idleness, knowing that you ought to be doing some important task; when you postpone some urgent duty because you "can't be bothered" or "don't feel up to it"; when you put off until to-morrow what you know ought to be done to-day – you are weakening your will. So don't say you are too tired or too busy or too nervous, but do it now and let your will-power reap the benefit.

74

Your aim, then, in developing a strong will must be to determine to accomplish every little task and duty that you know you ought to do but would rather avoid. Make up your mind to get up a little earlier in the morning, or to walk to business instead of riding, or to take up a hobby or physical exercises, or to give up smoking – or set yourself some other self-imposed task, it does not matter what it is so long as you determine to stick to it! Make up your mind to do a thing and do it, not because your life depends upon it, but because the fulfilling of any little task that may appear irksome, or the carrying out of an obligation which you are tempted to shirk, proves that you are not entirely devoid of will-power and determination, and it will result in a surprising improvement in your will-power in a very short time.

The accomplishment of any task, however insignificant, makes your Will a little strong than it was before.

PHYSICAL CULTURE. One of the finest aids in the banishment of a morbid and nervous disposition, and, indeed, any form of nerve-weakness, is physical culture. Not only does the regular daily practice of physical exercises develop will-power, but the movements themselves are very beneficial to the nerves. I strongly advise very reader who can do so to take up a course in simple physical training and to exercise regularly every day. The best systems are those which employ simple, natural movements – not strict military drill – and require no apparatus whatever.

I do not include a set of exercises in this Course because, firstly, this is a mental treatment and physical exercise is somewhat outside its province, and, secondly, because many of my older patients might be unable to carry out vigorous exercise. But I strongly recommend physical culture as a splendid stimulant for the nerves to all those who can take it up.

DURATION OF TREATMENT. Owing to the fact that nervous complaints differ widely in their intensity and character in every individual, it is, of course, impossible for me to give more than an approximate idea as to how long Suggestion will take to cure you. The length of treatment depends not only upon the intensity of your disorder, but also (and principally) upon the energy and enthusiasm you put into the practice of Suggestion. From past experience I have found that long-standing and severe cases are by no means the most difficult to cure, as success depends more upon the enthusiasm the patient puts into his effects than upon the extent of his nervous condition.

In the preceding pages of this Course I have done my utmost to convince you that if you will only persevere and put your whole energy into the persistent practice of Suggestion, the prospects of a cure are absolutely certain. Correctly and earnestly applied, Suggestion cannot fail and in every case a cure is a question of time only. The average time required to effect a cure in most cases is two to six weeks, but you must be prepared to continue the treatment for a long period if your own particular case demands it.

Some remarkably rapid cures have been effected under the Rivers treatment, indeed, many sufferers have told me that they felt so relieved and elated after reading the Course that they even found it unnecessary to use the Suggestion Tables at all! This is not so remarkable as it at first seems when it is realised that whereas a bodily wound or a diseased or injured organ may take months to heal, an imaginary complaint or a groundless hallucination may, when properly understood, be expelled from the mind instantaneously.

Whether your cure takes a few hours or a few weeks depends entirely upon you.

TREATMENT OF SEVERAL COMPLAINTS. Should you be suffering from several nervous complaints it is not advisable to treat more than one complaint at a time unless your condition is so bad that this arrangement would considerably prolong the duration of treatment. Many nervous fears and mental disorders are closely allied and the eradication of one complaint will have the effect of automatically dispelling other similar afflictions. The practice of the Suggestion Table for Self-consciousness will cure all the symptoms of a self-conscious disposition, such as Shyness, Nervousness, Timidity, Embarrassment, Bashfulness, etc. The use of the Table for Morbid Fears will dispel all forms of fear with which you may be afflicted, even though you apply Suggestion to only one form of fear.

If you are suffering from several forms of nerve-weakness I advise you to treat your worst complaint first and not commence the treatment of another complaint until you are at least well on the way to a cure in the case of the first complaint. Should you be afflicted with so many nervous disorders that you cannot wait until one symptom is cured before treating another, you may use Suggestion Tables for two complaints each day arranging the times of practice as far apart as possible.

FINAL WORDS. My task is now finished! On looking back over the work I have done, while I cannot say that I am thoroughly satisfied with its literary standard, I nevertheless believe that I have succeeded in what I set out to accomplish, namely, to give you all the advice and assistance in curing yourself that another person could possibly render.

I hope you now quite understand that the curing of your complaint rests entirely upon your own shoulders. No other person can cure you, but you can cure yourself however nervous you are. The only assistance that a second person can give in such cases is to show you how to cure yourself, and this is what I have tried to do in writing this Course of Treatment. Again let me assure you that if only you will persevere and give Suggestion sufficient time to get into proper working order, this Treatment will cure you – as it has cured thousands of other sufferers all over the world.

I am sure you will appreciate that this Course if written solely for the benefit of my patients and I hope you will regard the information imparted to you as private and confidential and treat it accordingly. The Rivers Course of Treatment is supplied on the condition that it must not be re-sold or used by any other person than the actual patient to whom it is supplied, which I am sure you will agree is only fair to you as the purchaser and to me as the author of the Course. If you do not wish to keep these little books after you have completed the treatment I ask you kindly to destroy them.

In the foregoing pages of this Course I have explained in very simple language what Suggestion is and its method of application, but it must be understood that I have merely touched the border of this great power. Of the immense possibilities of Psychotherapy I have said very little. I have simply stated such facts as it is necessary you should know without making any attempt to enter upon a scientific explanation of them. I have told you just sufficient about Psychotherapeutic treatment that the curing of your disorder necessitated, entirely avoiding the scientific and theoretical aspects of the subject, as they need not concern the sufferer.

I now place into your hand the key to a brighter, healthier and happier future – a time when the intense misery of a nervous temperament will be buried in the past and a cheerful, fearless and confident disposition take its place. The key of the fetters that bind you, that drag you down and pinion you to the walls of misery and failure, is now in your hands – make use of it and free yourself while you have the opportunity!

Confident that I have now done all that I can do towards effecting your cure, I must now leave you to work alone. In bidding you goodbye and good luck, let me finally impress upon you the necessity of being determined, patient and cheerful. Just pin your faith to Suggestion, practise regularly, believe in your ability to cure yourself and you cannot possibly fail.

SUGGESTION TABLE NO. 1

DEPRESSION, ANXIETY, WORRY, etc.

Once (Mentally) :
I am no longer worried or depressed.

Four Times (Whispering) :
Nothing upsets me now; I can stand any trouble without getting worried or depressed.

Three Times (Softly) :
Troubles and difficulties never last long. It is absurd to worry over things that cannot be avoided.

Twice (Softly) :
I feel radiantly happy and contented, I do not feel in the least depressed.

Once (Aloud) :
Life is worth living when one can feel as free from worry and depression as I do. All my old depression has quite gone – I feel wonderfully happy now!

SUGGESTION TABLE NO. 2

IMAGINARY FEARS & DELUSIONS.

Once (Mentally) :
I am afraid of nothing! I have no imaginary fear, no stupid delusions, no illness, no worries, no troubles.

Six Times (Whispering) :
I am well and happy. I am sound in body and mind.

Three Times (Softly) :
I am not in the least worried about the future. I am not concerned about my health. Nothing can cause me a single moment's misgiving.

Twice (Softly) :
All my former fears have been dispelled, I haven't a particle of fear now.

Once (Aloud) :
How stupid of me to have worried so unnecessarily about nothing at all! I am ashamed to think I allowed my imagination to make such a fool of me. Suggestion has completely killed all my silly fears.

SUGGESTION TABLE NO. 3

FEAR OF BECOMING INSANE.

Once (Mentally) :
I no longer fear that my mind is becoming unsound. That absurd idea was sheer imagination.

Four Times (Whispering) :
My brain is perfectly sound. There is nothing whatever wrong with my mind.

Three Times (Softly) :
I have complete control of myself; I never think or act strangely.

Twice (Softly) :
I am in full possession of my faculties.

Once (Aloud) :
It is quite impossible for me to lose my reason because I have sufficient will-power to keep my mind completely under control. I cannot go insane unless I let myself go – which I never will! I am quite cured of the stupid fear of insanity.

SUGGESTION TABLE NO. 4

FOR SUICIDAL TENDENCIES.

Once (Mentally) :
I have quite conquered the wicked desire to end my life. I never have such terrible thoughts now.

Four Times (Whispering) :
I am far too happy and too ambitious to want to die yet!

Three Times (Softly) :
I have everything to live for; I want to live and enjoy life – and I am going to!

Twice (Softly) :
The terrible shock and pain that such a cowardly act would inflict upon my relatives and friends is too awful to think of.

Once (Aloud) :
May God forgive me for ever entertaining such a shocking idea! I will never think of such terrible things again. It is glorious to know that I have completely mastered the horrible desire for death.

SUGGESTION TABLE NO. 5

FEAR OF STORMS.

Once (Mentally) :
I am no longer afraid of thunder and lightning.

Three Times (Whispering) :
The heaviest storm does not alarm me now.

Three Times (Softly) :
Lightning is a harmless electrical discharge and thunder is about as dangerous as a penny cracker – I don't care a rap about either!

Twice (Softly) :
How absurd to be scared of harmless elements! I like to watch a display of lightning.

Once (Aloud) :
All my old fear of thunderstorms has quite gone – if ever I WAS afraid, but I can't believe that I was ever so foolish. Neither the most vivid lightning nor the loudest peal of thunder would make me turn a hair now!

SUGGESTION TABLE NO. 6

INSOMNIA

Once (Mentally) :
I shall sleep soundly to-night and not wake until morning.

Four Times (Whispering) :
I can hardly keep my eyes open – I am absolutely tired out.

Three Times (Softly) :
I shall be fast asleep almost as soon as I have finished by Suggestion Table.

Three Times (Softly) :
I AM tired to-night.

Once (Aloud) :
Now I have finished Suggestion and I am going to sleep at once. In a few minutes I shall be fast asleep.

SUGGESTION TABLE NO. 7

SELF-CONSCIOUSNESS.

Once (Mentally) :
I am no longer nervous and shy. I am afraid of nothing and nobody.

Four Times (Whispering) :
My old nervousness has quite gone.

Three Times (Softly) :
I don't know that it is to blush or feel shy now.

Twice (Softly) :
I can speak to anyone without the slightest suspicion of embarrassment.

Once (Aloud) :
I am quite cool and composed under all circumstances. Nothing and nobody can make me embarrassed or confused because I have now sufficient will-power to prevent it. Thank God I can now enjoy life without that horrible feeling making a fool of me. All my nervousness was stupid imagination – nothing more!

SUGGESTION TABLE NO. 8

STOP SMOKING

Once (Mentally) :
I AM going to stop smoking.

Four Times (Whispering) :
It is so unnatural to inhale damaging smoke into by body.

Three Times (Softly) :
My life would be so much better if I did not smoke.

Twice (Softly) :
I shall never smoke again because my will-power is too strong to allow this to happen.

Once (Aloud) :
I feel so much better now that I have stopped smoking. It was an expensive, harmful and stupid thing to have done. I feel great now in so many ways.

SUGGESTION TABLE NO. 9

NERVOUS HEADACHE (AND OTHER NERVE PAINS).

Once (Mentally) :
My head does not ache now.

Six Times (Whispering) :
The pain has quite gone!

Three Times (Softly) :
I can't feel the slightest pain anywhere! I must have imagined I had a headache, I have no trace of it now.

Twice (Softly) :
Wonderful how that pain vanished so quickly!

Once (Aloud) :
That headache was pure imagination. I feel as fit as a fiddle and have not a pain in my body!

SUGGESTION TABLE NO. 10

SUPPLEMENTARY TABLE.

Once (Mentally) :
I am quite cured now! Since taking up Auto-Suggestion my former nervousness has quite gone!

Three Times (Whispering) :
I have completely mastered my emotions. I simply CANNOT feel nervous now.

Three Times (Softly) :
How grand to be so confident and composed under any circumstances!

Twice (Softly) :
Suggestion has made a man of me! I am no longer nervous, depressed or worried. I feel splendid!

Once (Aloud) :
It is really wonderful what a remarkable improvement Suggestion has made upon me. It is difficult to believe that only a few weeks ago I was so nervous and depressed and now I am as fit and as confident as anyone. I feel a new man! I am radiantly happy – my cure is complete!

www.ingramcontent.com/pod-product-compliance
Lightning Source LLC
Chambersburg PA
CBHW021625270326
41931CB00008B/871